CLOSE THE APP MAKE THE TING

INTRODUCTION

1987-2009

I was born in July 1987 in Hackney to Jamaican parents. I still live in East London today, and this is the lens I've experienced the world through. I grew up with culture on my doorstep, some publicly funded and a lot run by independent passionate people and organisations that I'm a beneficiary of. I didn't even notice it, it was just my normal, until some of those support structures began to collapse under austerity. My interests have always been wide, but pirate radio was the constant throughout my early life. I listened to Reggae, Jungle, Garage then what became known as Grime emerged in my early teens as I was figuring out what I wanted to do with my life. At the same time an internet revolution was happening, the early days of Napster that could give you access to any song you wanted for the first time, forums where you could talk to others listening to the same pirate radio shows, then later the early stages of social media gave me the sense the world was changing fast. I spent my teenage years online writing blogs and on forums curious about how all of this would impact music, and how I could get involved.

Grime was the spark to take creative work seriously. The music felt like a combination of all of the sounds I grew up listening to, led by MCs that had big characters that had the potential to change what the country looked and sounded like. The scene developing in my area was promising, but I couldn't figure out my role in it. I had this idea of being somewhere between a DJ and a journalist in 2005, but I took what I thought would be a safe route and went to University and studied Business.

The only useful thing that came out of University was meeting Skilliam, a friend who later became my creative partner. I graduated in 2009, at the height of the global financial crisis, and couldn't get a job. It was a chance to give my idea of being a 'DJ and journalist' a try four years later. Skilliam and I joined Rinse FM, the station I had listened to some of my favourite artists on, and it felt like the chance to do something special.

2010-2019

After a year of shows on Rinse FM playing new Grime music, we needed a vessel for all the music we were being sent, and new artists we were meeting. At the time the scene was in a strange place, the artists I grew up listening to were making bad pop records, as their authentic music got no industry support. Record shops were closing rapidly and vinyl sales, which at their height for some artists were upwards of 5000+ a release, were down to 300 sales. Then there were hardly any club nights dedicated to the music, because of a racist policy by the Metropolitan Police called Form 696 that let them cancel any event they deemed 'high risk' at any time based on who was performing, or the majority ethnicity of the attendees.

We started Butterz the label to give a home to special producers of the music that didn't want to make bad pop songs, wanted to DJ in clubs, and wanted to have their music on vinyl. Skilliam and I had no industry experience, we just reverse engineered the process of what we thought made sense which got us a long way, and had help from many that could see our vision for what we wanted the scene to be.

When thinking about the branding for the label, I wanted to have something stripped back, as I thought a lot of the artwork in the scene was bad. When researching the costs to press our first record it said full colour artwork was £700 to print, then two colours was £500. We only had £500 to start off with, and I chose black and yellow. That is why this book is black and yellow too.

For a small operation, with niche music, in a rapidly changing music landscape Butterz was a success. We got to release music with some of our favourite MCs like JME, Flowdan, D Double E, Footsie and P Money, we built a musical family with Royal-T, Swindle, Flava D, DJ Q at its core that extended much wider, and we got to travel the world, playing shows and making music with artists from every continent.

Skilliam and I's roles shifted away from DJ's more into artist and project management, and the core label idea felt complete, we planned to close the label in 2020 with final releases, parties and a grant to help emerging artists start their own labels. Then 2020 happened.

2020-2024

Focusing on only the positives of 2020 into 2021, lockdown gave me a chance to reflect on what I had done so far, and if I even wanted to continue on this path. I deactivated my social media accounts, not realising you lose your account and followers after 30 days. Losing all the followers I built in the previous decade felt fresh, but what do you say online with no followers?

Everything reopened in July 2021, and I had been tweeting my thoughts about what the creative scene could be after lockdown, and DJ Jubilee said I should put the writing on Instagram. I never used it seriously before that, but I drew out some of the first ideas you will see in this book on paper, and just posted them. They got maybe two or three comments, which was enough to continue. I bought an iPad with an Apple Pencil, got a free app called Procreate and made tidier versions in Black and Yellow, and that was the beginning of what became the 'Yellow Square'. Short sharp ideas on creativity, scenes and where I felt independent music was going.

Three years, and hundreds of squares later, I've compiled the best of the ideas in this book as a set of creative prompts that may help you when you are unsure of what to do next. This isn't advice, it's a way to spark your own ideas.

The 'in theory' half is inspired by all the years of working in Grime, the conversations I've had with many of you in direct messages and at events in person. It's also a way of preserving the writing outside of the apps, which in the grand scheme of things will be a temporary fixture in our lives.

The 'in practice' half is the projects that I've created based on the ideas within the squares. These have taken the writing outside of social media, and put it into the real world in a way that was fun, low cost and on the fly. Nothing in this has had heavy planning, just flow.

The best feedback I can get from this book is not a positive review, it's seeing what you made because of it. So for now, Close the app, read the ting, and I'll check back in with you at the end of the book.

Elijah

IN THEORY

SCENE

(DEAD SCENE)

IT'S NOT AN ECOSYSTEM IF EVERYONE IS DOING THE SAME THING

IT'S A CREATIVE ECOSYSTEM WHEN EVERYONE BUILDS DIFFERENT IDEAS WITH THE SAME PRINCIPLES

1/1

>

#1

MAKE ZERO YOUR FAVOURITE NUMBER

HOW CAN I GET PAID TO MAKE WHATEVER I LIKE, WITH PEOPLE ENJOYING IT WITHOUT ME HAVING TO PROMOTE IT, WHILE LIVING AN ABOVE STANDARD OF LIVING IN ONE OF THE MOST EXPENSIVE CITIES?

THE ANSWER TO MOST QUESTIONS IN MY WORK: I DON'T KNOW, LET'S TRY IT.

STOP TELLING PEOPLE TO 'JUST WORK HARD'

IF YOU GREW UP IN A WORKING CLASS HOUSEHOLD YOU KNOW HARD WORK DOESN'T ALWAYS PAY OFF

TIME IS THE CREATIVE DIRECTOR

DOOMSCROLL FORMULA

1. LOOK AT YOUR WEEKLY SCREEN TIME
2. MULTIPLY BY 52 TO ANNUALISE
3. MINUS YOUR AGE VS 80 (AVERAGE LIFE EXPECTANCY)
4. MULTIPLY STEPS 2+3
5. CLOSE THE APP
5. MAKE THE TING

HOW DIFFERENT WOULD YOUR PROJECT, LABEL OR COLLECTIVE BE IF YOU SET A ONE YEAR LIMIT?

MORE
TIME
YOU
DON'T
NEED
MORE
TIME

SOCIAL
MEDIA

IS
A

CANVAS
CANVAS
CANVAS
CANVAS

NOT

AN

ADVERTISING
ADVERTISING

BOARD

USE IT
IN THE
MOST

ARTISTIC
WAY
POSSIBLE

ソーシャル・メディアは

IDEA | VIDEO | SONG

CONTEXT | COLLAB | QUESTION

WIP | HISTORY | MEME

キャンバスだ

ARE YOU TRYING TO BE DISCOVERED IN THE WAY YOU DISCOVER TINGS YOURSELF?

HIGH FOLLOWER COUNT IS BECOMING A NEGATIVE INDICATOR

DEEP FEEDBACK □

1. AN ARTISTIC RESPONSE
2. HIGH EFFORT COMMENT, REVIEW OR DISCUSSION
3. PRIVATE RECOMMENDATION

DO YOU WANT A FIRE EMOJI & A PRE SAVE OR DO YOU WANT TEARS IN THE CLUB?

MAKE YOUR POINTS WITH THE SMALL NUMBERS:

I GOT 100 PEOPLE IN THE ROOM > HAVING 10,000 FOLLOWERS.

MAKE YOUR POINTS
WITH THE SMALL
NUMBERS:
ME & 3 FRIENDS
MADE SOMETHING >
MY COMMUNITY HAS
1000 MEMBERS

DON'T TRUST THE PROCESS TEST THE PROCESS

その過程こそが
アートだろ

IMPOSTER SYNDROME IS A FEATURE NOT A BUG

ART IS
MAKING
WITHIN
YOUR
MEANS

FASTEST ROUTE INTO THE CREATIVE INDUSTRY 2024:

LEARN THE MOST FREQUENTLY LISTED SKILLS ON JOB DESCRIPTIONS.

GET ANY JOB YOU CAN. LEARN AS MUCH AS POSSIBLE FROM THE INSIDE. FIGURE OUT WAYS TO BE USEFUL OUTSIDE OF YOUR JOB DESCRIPTION

WORK ON YOUR OWN PROJECTS IN YOUR FREE TIME. USE THE LEARNING IN YOUR DAY JOB. MORE WORK OPTIONS SHOULD OPEN UP.

BASIC DESIGN & VIDEO EDITING BRING A LOT OF VALUE TO ENTRY LEVEL ROLES. PRACTICE WITH YOUR OWN PROJECTS

CONSISTENT INCOME MEANS YOUR ART PROJECTS AREN'T UNDER PRESSURE TO MAKE MONEY. USE THIS FREEDOM TO EXPERIMENT & BUILD CONNECTIONS

* YOU CAN GET PAID BETTER IN OTHER INDUSTRIES DOING SIMILAR WORK.
* CONTRIBUTING TO SOCIETY IN OTHER WAYS WILL INSPIRE DIFFERENT ART.

IF YOUR PROJECT BLOWS UP YOU CAN LEAVE YOUR JOB. YOUR SKILLS WILL STILL HAVE VALUE AS A FREELANCER.

BEING AN ARTIST 'FULL TIME' DOESN'T HAVE TO BE THE GOAL. FINDING A WAY THAT WORKS FOR YOU IS.

INFRASTRUCTURAL CHALLENGES IN ELECTRONIC MUSIC:

HOW DOES AN ECOSYSTEM FUNCTION WITH 100 x THE ARTISTS?

WHO ARE THE NEXT GENERATION OF PROMOTERS?

COST TO PUT ON SHOWS HAS RISEN BUT TICKET PRICES HAVEN'T. IT'S LOW MARGIN + HIGH RISK.

WHY DO IT?

IS A CLUB NIGHT STILL THE BEST WAY TO CONNECT LIKEMINDED ARTISTS IN 2024?

IT'S NOT AN ECOSYSTEM IF EVERYONE IS DOING THE SAME THING

IT'S A CREATIVE ECOSYSTEM WHEN WE BUILD DIFFERENT IDEAS WITH THE SAME PRINCIPLES & ETHICS

THE WORLD MOVES TOO FAST FOR LONG TERM DEALS. IF A LABEL HAS NO STUDIO, NOT INVESTING ANY MONEY AND DOESN'T HAVE EVENTS. WHY ARE YOU GIVING AWAY THE RIGHTS TO YOUR MUSIC?

E.P FORMAT DOES NOT FIT WITH MODERN CONSUMPTION LOOK AT PUBLIC STATISTICS

SINGLES GET 100x THE PLAYS

VINYL: TOO SLOW & EXPENSIVE. SHIPPING + TAX KILL REST OF WORLD DEMAND. DJs & CLUBS NO LONGER PRIORITISE IT. DIY LABELS LOSE MONEY ON MOST PRESSINGS.

THERE IS AN OVERSATURATION **OF 'RADIO' CONTENT**

HOW MANY PEOPLE ARE LISTENING? WHY IS FREE LABOUR OK IN RADIO? HOW DOES THIS SERVE THE CREATORS OF THE MUSIC? WHAT IS THE OPPORTUNITY COST?

ARE THERE OTHER STRUCTURES THAT CAN BE BUILT?

OF THE ARTISTS THAT MAKE MONEY MOST DON'T MAKE ENOUGH TO BE ABLE TO REINVEST FAST ENOUGH TO STAY HOT. THIS IS WHY NEW IDEAS SLOW WHEN AN ARTIST BLOWS UP. THE FINANCIAL GAP BETWEEN HOW MUCH ARTISTS GET PAID ON THE SAME LINE UP MEANS ARTISTS CAN BE VISIBLE BUT NOT FINANCIALLY VIABLE.

WHAT IS THE DIFFERENCE **WHEN A** PLATFORM · LABEL RADIO STATION BOOKING AGENCY GOES FROM 30 ARTISTS TO 100 ARTISTS? WHAT IDEAS STILL SERVE ARTISTS AT SCALE? IF ARTISTS OPT OUT OF THESE SYSTEMS WHAT HAPPENS NEXT?

WHAT DO YOU WANT A MANAGER TO DO?

ALL MANAGERS HAVE DIFFERENT SKILLS & WORKING STYLE.

WRITE WHAT YOU THINK YOU NEED AS A JOB DESCRIPTION.

YOU DON'T NEED A MANAGER TO:

- MAKE MUSIC
- BUILD AN AUDIENCE
- GET FUNDING
- DO SHOWS
- SIGN DEALS
- START A LABEL

AGENTS DON'T GET YOU BOOKINGS

DOING AS MUCH
AS YOU CAN BY
YOURSELF WILL
HELP YOU PICK A
GOOD PARTNER

NEW MUSIC WON'T BLOW THROUGH OLD DISTRIBUTION

WOULD YOU CHANGE THE FORMAT IF IT MEANT MORE PEOPLE HEARD YOUR MUSIC?

MORE OF US NEED TO TEAM UP. SHARE RESOURCES. JOINT SHOWS. ARTIST OWNED MEDIA. TEMPORARY CREWS. INTERGENERATIONAL COLLECTIVES...

YOU CAN INSULATE YOURSELF WITH PROFESSIONALS LIKE MANAGERS + AGENTS + LABELS.

BUT IT IS STILL HARD TO BREAK WITHOUT LIKEMINDED ARTISTS ORBITING YOUR WORK

FRIENDS
BUY
TICKETS

A ONE DIMENSIONAL VIEW ON WHAT FRIENDSHIP CAN BE HELD ME BACK FOR A LOT OF MY LIFE

NONE OF
MY MENTORS
KNOW THEY
ARE MY
MENTORS

SAYING THE WORD 'LOVE' TO THE MAN DEM IS GOOD FOR EVERYONES MENTAL HEALTH

LEAVE THOUGTFUL COMMENTS ON ART THAT MOVES YOU.

YOU AREN'T TRYING TO REACH AS MANY PEOPLE AS POSSIBLE

IMAGINE THE WORLD IF BLACK PEOPLE HAD BEEN PAID FAIRLY FOR THEIR ART

IF YOU ONLY LISTEN TO MUSIC IN ENGLISH, YOU ARE ONLY DABBLING WITH MUSIC

WHAT HAPPENED TO ____?

THEY GOT BURNED OUT

THEY ARE STILL CREATING BUT NOT SHARING

THE FINANCIAL STRESS BECAME TOO MUCH

FAMILY PRIORITIES

GOT SCAMMED

WORK BEHIND THE SCENES

PEOPLE HATED THEIR LAST PROJECT AND IT MADE THEM QUIT

THEY SAID ALL THEY WANTED TO

THEIR SCENE WAS DECLARED 'DEAD'

GIVE ARTISTS SPACE
TO MAKE WORK
YOU DON'T FEEL
WITHOUT DECIDING
YOU DON'T LIKE
THEM ANYMORE

MUSIC IS FREE.
THE MUSIC INDUSTRY
IS A MONOPOLY.

IF THEY BELIEVE IT THEY WILL WRITE ABOUT IT FOR FREE

YOU DON'T NEED A MARKETING PLAN. DEVELOP A STRATEGY YOU CAN DO AT LOW COST CONSISTENTLY THAT'S FLEXIBLE, FUN PROMOTES YOUR ART AUTHENTICALLY.

YOU DON'T NEED PR. DO NOT DELEGATE AUDIENCE BUILDING. NOBODY WANTS TO BE ADVERTISED TO. WHAT WOULD MAKE YOU SHARE OR BUY WHAT YOU POSTED?

IT TAKES
A VILLAGE
TO RAISE
AN ARTIST.

CULTURE WAS THE WORD OF THE 10s COMMUNITY IS THE WORD OF THE 20s

IF YOU LOVE MUSIC YOU SHOULD LEARN HOW TO DJ

DISCONNECT DJING (PLAYING WITH MUSIC) FROM BEING A DJ (WORKING IN MUSIC) EXPLORE THE JOY OF CURATING YOURSELF

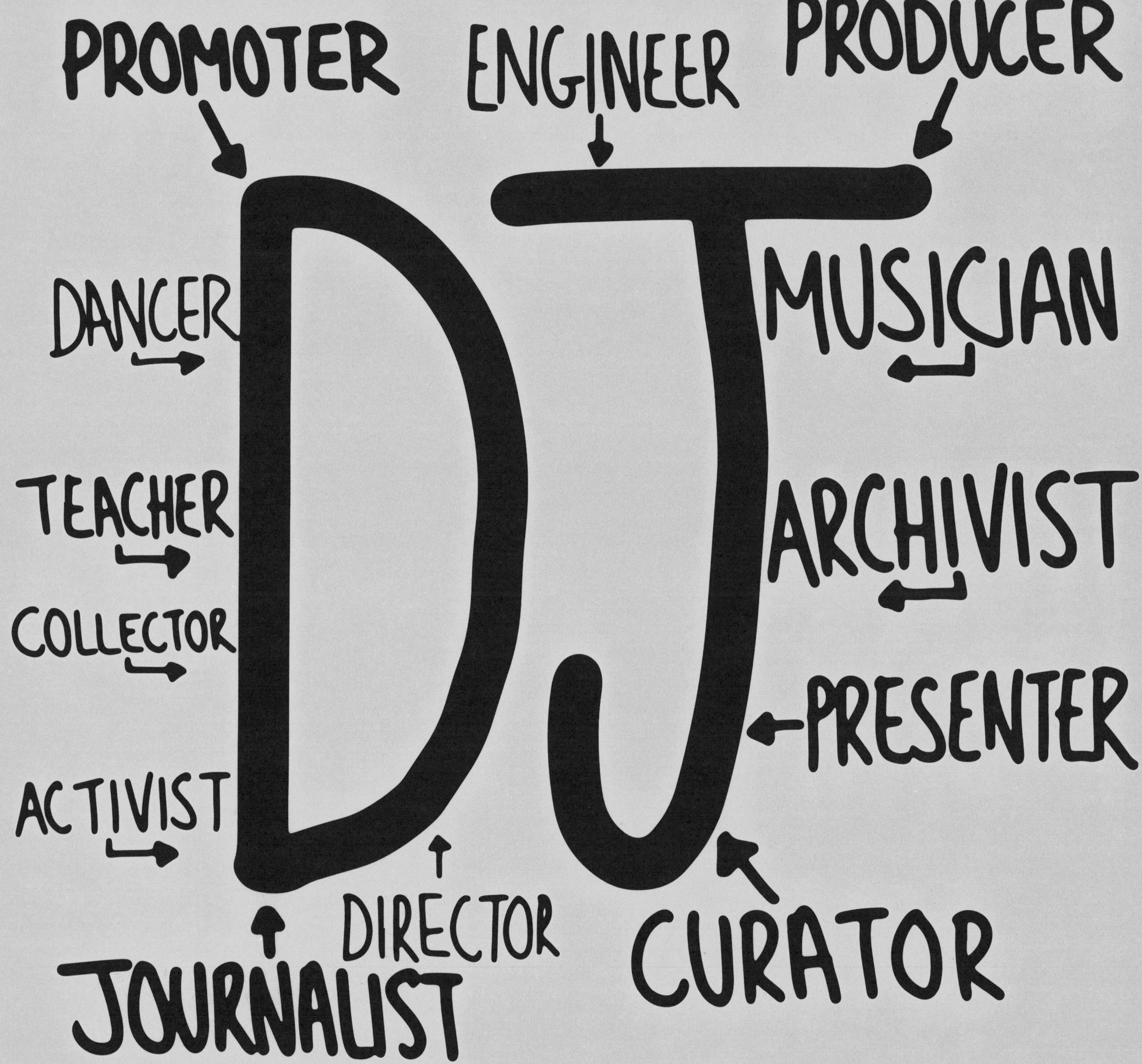

PROMOTER ENGINEER PRODUCER

DJ

DANCER

MUSICIAN

TEACHER

ARCHIVIST

COLLECTOR

PRESENTER

ACTIVIST

DIRECTOR

JOURNALIST

CURATOR

THERE AREN'T ENOUGH DJs

REMIX:
ALTERNATIVE VERSION BY PRIMARY ARTIST.

ORIGINAL WORK COMMISSIONED BY ARTIST OR LABEL.

DUB: VERSION WITH STRIPPED BACK VOCALS.

DUBPLATE: UNRELEASED OR EARLY VERSION. 1/1 RECORDING FOR DJ.

EDIT: VARIATION IN PRODUCTION NOT FROM ORIGINAL ARTIST. + STRUCTURAL CHANGE FROM ORIGINAL ARTIST.

VIP: VARIATION IN PRODUCTION FROM ORIGINAL ARTIST.
* VERSION MADE FOR SELECTED DJs.

BOOTLEG:
UNOFFICIAL REMIX DONE WITHOUT ARTIST / LABEL PERMISSION

* USUALLY WITHOUT STEMS
* SOMETIMES THEY GET OFFICIAL RELEASE

D*VIL MIX *TERM COINED BY WILEY
INSTRUMENTAL VERSION WITH NO DRUMS. INSPIRED BY KING TUBBY + DUB REGGAE

I.D: ONLINE SHORT FORM FOR UNRECOGNISABLE OR UNRELEASED SONG.

* I.D + DUBPLATE SOMETIMES MEAN THE SAME THING

MASH UP:
TWO EXISTING SONGS COMBINED TO MAKE NEW ONE.

MOST NEVER SEE OFFICIAL RELEASE

SO ANTI
ALGORITHM
IT MIGHT*
BANG!

THE PERCEPTION OF DIGITAL PERMANENCE HAS TAKEN THE SPONTANEITY OUT OF MUSIC.

NAME AN ARTIST THAT HAS MADE MORE THAN 100 SONGS YOU LOVE

THEY DON'T CARE WHAT THE GENRE IS, THEY JUST WANT A GOOD SONG.

HAS THERE EVER BEEN A CREATIVE SCENE THAT HAS THRIVED UNDER HIGH RENT?

RENT IS THE CREATIVE DIRECTOR!

THE STYLE IS THE SIGNATURE

ALIENATING

>

STAGNATING

ARTISTS ARE NOT CONTENT CREATORS*

CONTENT IS MADE WITH THE INTENT TO PUBLISH

HOW TO'S WON'T HELP YOU WHERE WE ARE GOING

ONLINE ALL THE TIME = PESSIMISTIC

OFFLINE ALL THE TIME = OPTIMISTIC

THE MUSIC DOESN'T GET BETTER OR WORSE. YOU CHANGE.

YOU CAN BE A SPECIALIST WITHOUT BEING A PURIST

INTERESTING CITIES CAN'T BE QUIET!

MUSIC PLAYING LOUD FROM CARS USED TO BE A LOCAL SURVEY OF WHAT'S POPPING

HALF ANALOGUE
HALF DIGITAL
HALF ANALOGUE
HALF DIGITAL
HALF ANALOGUE
HALF DIGITAL

THE IDEA
THAT CREATES
THE IDEAS
THAT CREATES
THE IDEAS

DOING THE IDEA YOU CAN GET DONE WITH LOW STRESS DOESN'T MEAN IT CAN'T HAVE HIGH UPSIDE!

A GOOD IDEA IN
LONDON
MAY NOT BE
A GOOD IDEA IN

________________________________.

ARE THE IDEAS STILL TRUE AT SCALE? □

MAKE
OUTSIDE
THE
□

YOU HAVE TO
GO OUTSIDE
TO GET IT
DONE.
I'M SORRY.

IN PRACTICE

Close The App Make The Ting

This phrase became the container for all of the ideas that follow and where the name of the book came from. It was a response to a friend asking about what to do next creatively in a DM. There comes a point where all the strategy needs to go out of the window, none of the advice will help you, you need to just go.

I took my own direction, and started creating creative projects with the Yellow Square architecture from this point.

CLOSE
THE
APP
MAKE
THE
THING

Butterz
Record Label
2010-2021

Butterz was the record label I ran with Skilliam from 2010-2021. It was the right vessel for that period of time and for the music and artists it served, and I'm happy with what we contributed. Something that dominated my life for 11 years only having two pages in this book feels odd, but the Butterz and Grime story is for another time.

BUTTERZ
WAS
THE
LABEL

FABRICLIVE 8TH OCTOBER 2021
11PM-6AM

ROOM 1: BUTTERZ (A-Z)
ELIJAH & SKILLIAM · FLAVA D
FUMEZ THE ENGINEER · SWINDLE

ROOM 2: DAYTIMERS
D-LISH
DJ RITU
FRESHTA
KYLIN TYCE
YUNG SINGH

ROOM 3: VISA FREE
CHARISSE C
HAGAN
KG

TICKETS: FABRICLONDON.COM

YELLOW
BLACK
Butterz

YOUR
PLAN
ASSUMES
EVERYTHING
STAYS
THE
SAME

Yellow Square
Live

A hybrid lecture and music event concept at Outernet in Soho, September 2022. Producing this inspired all of the work outside of Instagram - the album with Jammz, the 360 installation, the billboards and the development of my lecture style.

DOCUMENT YOUR TING

Document Your Ting
Emma Warren B2B Elijah

A 'back to back' lecture based on Emma Warrens book 'Document Your Culture' at SOAS, May 2023. Dance is the physical embodiment of optimism and was inspired by reading Emma's book 'Dance Your Way Home'.

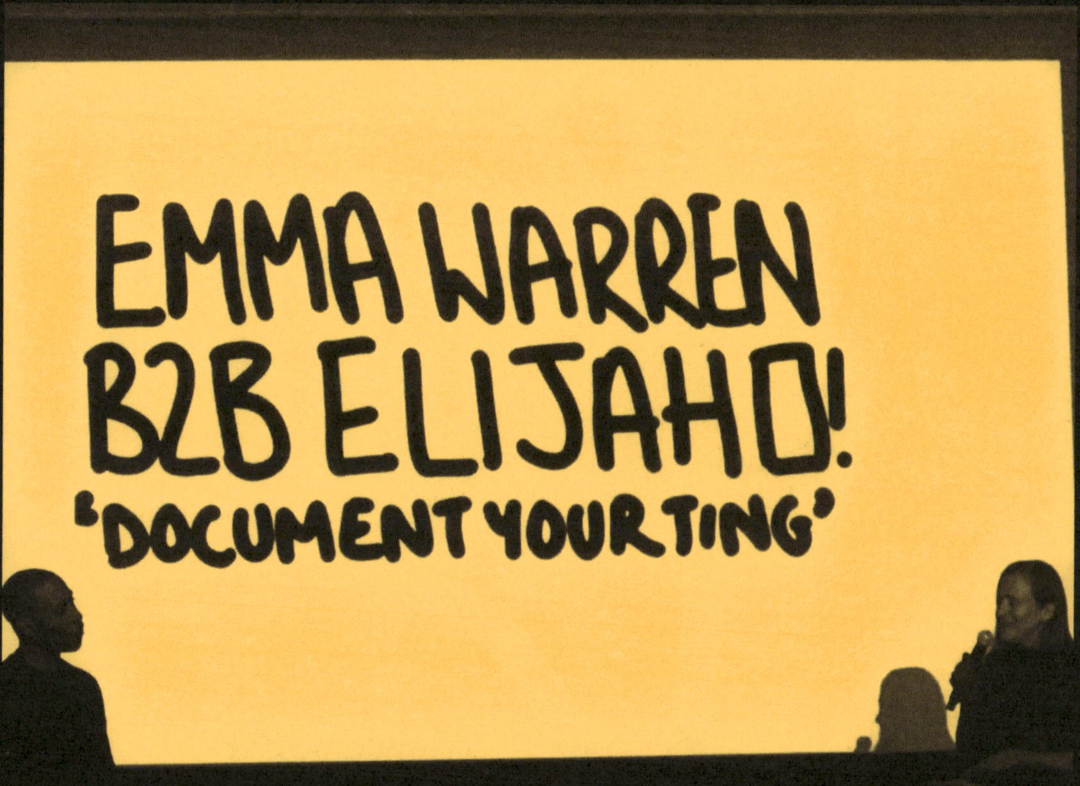

EMMA WARREN
B2B ELIJAH!
'DOCUMENT YOUR TING'

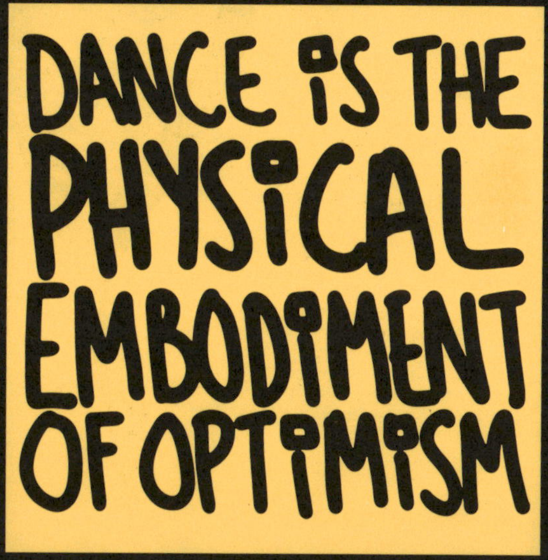

DANCE IS THE
PHYSICAL
EMBODIMENT
OF OPTIMISM

I collaborated with Grime MC Jammz to put the squares in musical form, and connect my writing back to my DJ sets. The first song we worked on together was over Blay Visions 'Cammy Riddim" which was a big instrumental track in the Grime scene in 2022. I asked Jammz about expanding this concept into a whole album, as long as we could do it really quickly. We did 3 zoom calls, exchanged hundreds of texts, and used a shared iPhone note to rebuild my concepts into songs across one week. Jammz recorded it in one day, then we released the acapella's before the official version came out so producers could remix it. I did a cover for everyone that sent me back a remix within 30 days, and let everyone release theirs themselves.

A few months later I came back to an idea I had in 2013, which was to release an album with a blank cover, and draw all the covers individually. So I did exactly that, and have created hundreds of physical yellow square covers for people that have bought the album directly from us on Bandcamp.

The collaboration with Jammz is just scratching the surface, and I hope to continue building on these ideas.

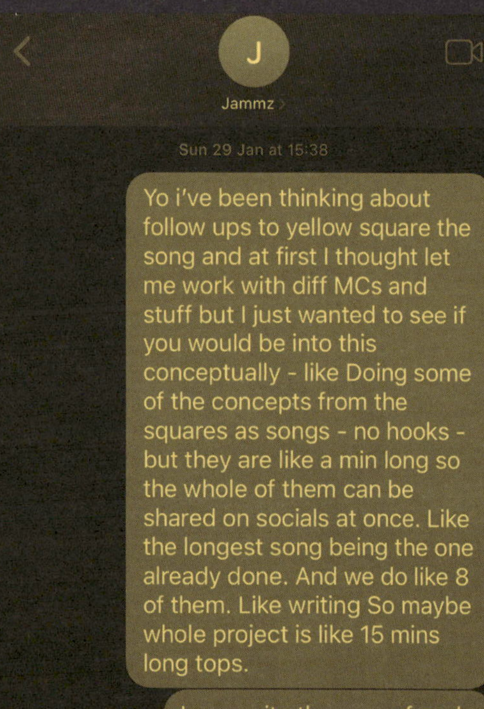

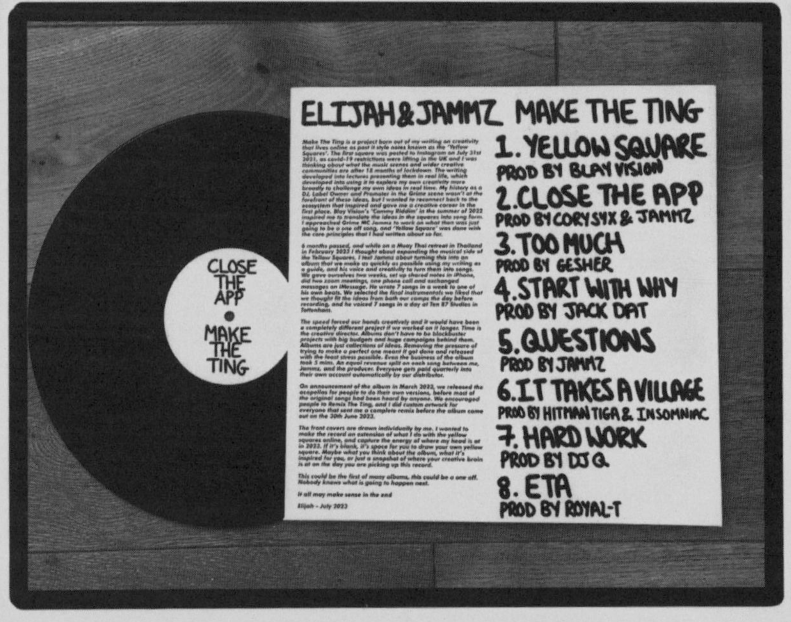

ELIJAH & JAMMZ MAKE THE TING
Make The Ting is a project born out of my writing on creativity that lives online as post it style notes known as the 'Yellow Squares'. The first square was posted to Instagram on July 31st 2021, as covid-19 restrictions were lifting in the UK and I was thinking about what the music scenes and wider creative communities are after 18 months of lockdown. The writing developed into lectures presenting them in real life, which developed into using it to explore my own creativity more broadly to challenge my own ideas in real time. My history as a DJ, Label Owner and Promoter in the Grime scene wasn't at the forefront of these ideas, but I wanted to reconnect back to the ecosystem that inspired and gave me a creative career in the first place. Blay Vision's 'Cammy Riddim' in the summer of 2022 inspired me to translate the ideas in the squares into song form. I approached Grime MC Jammz to work on what then was just going to be a one off song, and 'Yellow Square' was done with the core principles that I had written about so far.
6 months passed, and while on a Muay Thai retreat in Thailand in February 2023 I thought about expanding the musical side of the Yellow Squares. I text Jammz about turning this into an album that we make as quickly as possible using my writing as a guide, and his voice and creativity to turn them into songs. We gave ourselves two weeks, set up shared notes in iPhone, did two zoom meetings, one phone call and exchanged messages on iMessage. He wrote 7 songs in a week to one of his own beats. We selected the final instrumentals we liked that we thought fit the ideas from both our camps the day before recording, and he voiced 7 songs in a day at Ten 87 Studios in Tottenham.
The speed forced our hands creatively and it would have been a completely different project if we worked on it longer. Time is the creative director. Albums don't have to be blockbuster projects with big budgets and huge campaigns behind them. Albums are just collections of ideas. Removing the pressure of trying to make a perfect one meant it got done and released with the least stress possible. Even the business of the album took 5 mins. An equal revenue split on each song between me, Jammz, and the producer. Everyone gets paid quarterly into their own account automatically by our distributor.
On announcement of the album in March 2023, we released the acapellas for people to do their own versions, before most of the original songs had been heard by anyone. We encouraged people to Remix The Ting, and I did custom artwork for everyone that sent me a complete remix before the album came out on the 30th June 2023.
The front covers are drawn individually by me. I wanted to make the record an extension of what I do with the yellow squares online, and capture the energy of where my head is at in 2023. If it's blank, it's space for you to draw your own yellow square. Maybe what you think about the album, what it's inspired for you, or just a snapshot of where your creative brain is at on the day you are picking up this record.
This could be the first of many albums, this could be a one off. Nobody knows what is going to happen next.
It all may make sense in the end
Elijah – July 2023
1. YELLOW SQUARE
PROD BY BLAY VISION
2. CLOSE THE APP
PROD BY CORY SYX & JAMMZ
3. TOO MUCH
PROD BY GESHER
4. START WITH WHY
PROD BY JACK DAT
5. QUESTIONS
PROD BY JAMMZ
6. IT TAKES A VILLAGE
PROD BY HITMAN TIGA & INSOMNIAC
7. HARD WORK
PROD BY DJ Q
8. ETA
PROD BY ROYAL-T
CLOSE THE APP
MAKE THE TING

IF YOU ONLY LISTEN TO MUSIC IN ENGLISH YOU ARE ONLY DABBLING WITH MUSIC. BREAK FREE MAKE THE TING ☐ TO THE WORLD

USE YOUR OWN RULES FOR SUCCESS: MINE: TRY IDEAS OUT PUT THEM INTO THE WORLD, SEE WHAT HAPPENS, MAKE MORE, SHARE MY LEARNING AND REPEAT ☐! OCT 22ND 2023 @ELI1AH

ART IS MAKING WITHIN YOUR MEANS, BUT ALSO STRETCHING WHAT YOU THINK YOU ARE CAPABLE OF AND THE WORLD IS READY FOR. MAKE THE TING AND FIND OUT ☐! @ELI1AH · OCT 22ND 2023

CONNECTION > ENGAGEMENT DO WHAT YOU WOULD DO IF NOBOBY COULD SEE THE NUMBERS! @MAKETHETING OCTOBER 22ND 2023

DOCUMENT YOUR TING CREATE YOUR OWN LECTURE CAPTURE MOMENTS WHILE LIVING SHARING IS NOT ESSENTIAL BUT IT MAY CREATE DEEP FEEDBACK LOOPS THAT GIVE YOU MORE IDEAS ☐! @MAKE THE TING!

DJING HAS BEEN ______ HISTORICALLY. NOW TECHNOLOGY HAS CHANGED IT CAN BE ______. OCT 22ND 2023 · @ELI1AH ☐

MORE TIME } YOU DONT NEED MORE TIME
YOU DON'T NEED MORE } STUFF, MAKE WITH WHAT YOU HAVE
TIME MORE } DOESN'T ALWAYS HELP YOU
TIME → IS THE CREATIVE DIRECTOR
YOU → A 1 OF 1
DONT → WORRY ABOUT NUMBERS

LISTEN TO THIS BEFORE OPENING THE APP ☐! THEN CREATE YOUR OWN MUSIC, ART, LABEL, LECTURE, PARTY ☺
WRITTEN BY @ELI1AH 8TH NOVEMBER 2023 LONDON @MAKETHETING

THE CAMERA ROLL IS THE MOODBOARD. YOU SEE & HEAR UNIQUE TINGS EVERYDAY. USE THAT AS A CANVAS TO MAKE THE TING ☐ OCT 22ND 2023 · @ELI1AH

PRACTICE MAKES MORE TINGS
MORE TINGS MAKES MORE TINGS ☐ → @MAKE THE TING

CLOSE THE APP MAKE THE TING ☐

MAKE A LIST OF ALL THE TINGS YOU ARE OPTIMISTIC ABOUT. BUILD IDEAS WITH PEOPLE AROUND THESE PRINCIPLES. MAKE NEW TINGS ☐

SOME NEXT GUY
REMIXED
THE
TING □

PR□ PERC
MERC
THE
TING

IT TAKES A
VILLAGE TO
RAISE A
BOUKI□

ETA:
DESTINATION...
E.M.Z REMIX
"NEW CHALLENGES
COME WITH NEW
TERRAIN" □□□

TOO
MUCH
JAWLINE & NØELLE

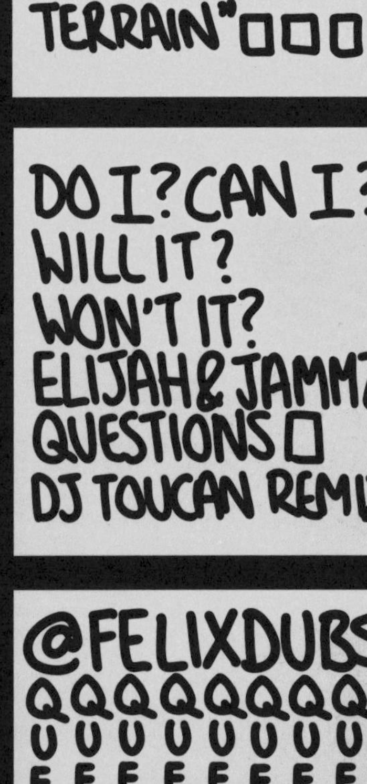

16 MINS
20 SECS
OF ♫ □
BY
KINKYBASS!

DJ ELIJAH & MC JAMMZ: LIVE 360

A LECTURE + DJ + MC SET HYBRID

DEC 1ST BRIGHTON

360
Brighton

I worked with Lighthouse and The Old Market in Brighton to develop a 360 version of the yellow square, which was part visual installation, part musical performance with Jammz and part lecture. Royal-T brought the album to life in a program called after effects that he was learning while producing this project and we had a couple of weeks to put it together. We were editing it right until doors opened and it's one of my best pieces of work I've been part of. Thanks to Bobby, Alli and the rest of the team that worked on it.

The Endz Is A Canvas

This served three functions:

1. Taking my ideas out of Instagram and putting them in the real world
2. Taking away advertising space from bad companies for a short time
3. Making me laugh

Special shouts to Build Hollywood, and my local club Leyton Orient for giving me the canvas.

Ask about space in your local areas for cool ideas and see what happens.

THE ENDZ IS A CANVAS

DJs
ARE
MUSIC
JOURNALISTS

Column for The Guardian, asking why 1xtra is failing Black British Music, June 2024. Journalism comes in many forms today, but I still think it's important to put my words in formats legible to those that still need the mainstream approval of ideas.

Opinion

Why are UK radio stations ignoring Black British music to play recycled American rap?

Elijah

We're already drowning in US pop culture. Surely there's a case for giving our homegrown talent a chance to compete

- Elijah is a DJ and writer specialising in Black British culture and electronic music

Wed 26 Jun 2024 10.00 BST

NY

São Paulo

The final release on Butterz was a vinyl edition of 'Brime!' by CESRV, Fleezus and Febem, a Brazilian Grime record that came out in 2021. It was amazing to commit their already cult classic project to wax, and I got to visit in February 2023, see them perform live, and do a lecture. Seeing 1000 people go mad for Grime in Brazil, what a dream.

I've been visiting Tokyo since 2014, while we were doing shows with the label, but hadn't been since 2018. The pandemic kept me out until I got to visit in March 2023, courtesy of Push Japan and FWB. This was the first time I did translations of the writing and I used mainly Japanese squares in the lecture.

I spent the first 3 months of 2023 nomadic, and this was the final trip before returning to London, which was emotional. I spent the final evening there walking through Tokyo in the rain listening to Ryuichi Sakamoto, and he passed away a couple of days later. Japan is a second home, and I'll always find a way back there.

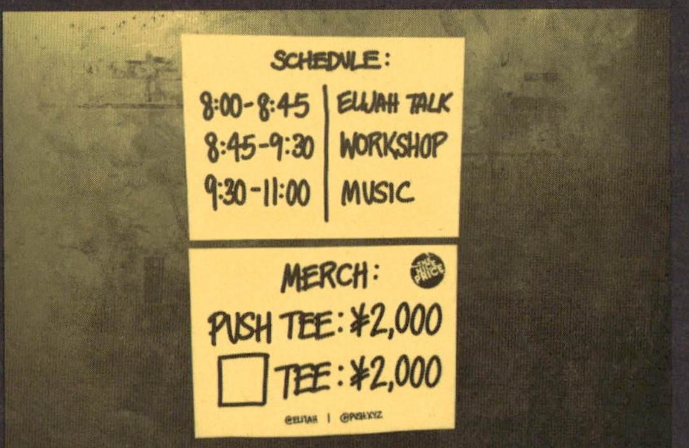

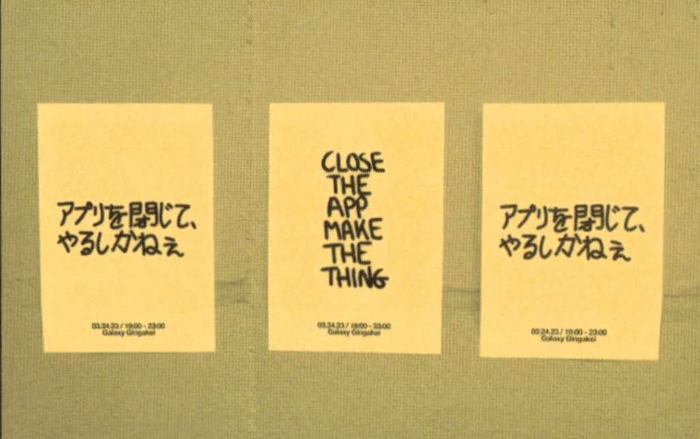

アプリを閉じて、
やるしかねぇ

THE PROCESS IS THE ART

Manila

Sai Versailles, a community leader, journalist and DJ from Manila reached out about coming to deliver a lecture in early 2023. My mentality with this project was I'd come everywhere that I was invited and that we found a feasible way to do an event, irrespective of fees. We worked on a proposal together, and the original funders fell through. I asked WeTransfer to support it, and it allowed us to do a joint lecture together, film it, and have other artists perform and share their work.

I finally made it in March 2024 and there was a great energy there, and Sai wrote these two squares that we discussed in the lecture that I wanted to include here because I think they are special thoughts to put into print.

UNDER WHAT CIRCUMSTANCES SHOULD ART NOT BE PURSUED?

HOW DO WE IMPROVE DISCOURSE WHEN CONTEXT IS CONSTANTLY OBSCURED?

World Tour

I did lectures across the world in 2023 and 2024. The squares are drawn by people that came to the event in Hong Kong, and the pictures are from my tour in India.

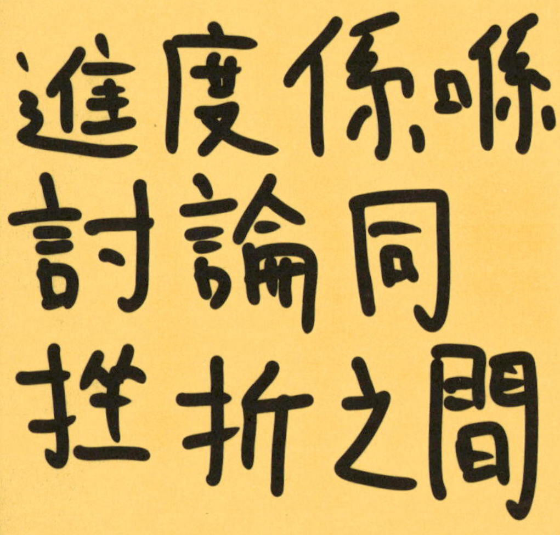

乜都係
實驗

IF YOU
LOVE MUSIC
YOU SHOULD
TO DJ

TONIGHT
THANK YOU
SEEDCENTRAAL!
IT TAKES A
GLOBAL VILLAGE

INDORE
ACCELLERATION
DJ ACCELLERATIONISM
MOVE FAST. MAKE TINGS

THE TING
AANCHAL!?

ENOUGH
CLOSE THE APP
KONNEKT THE
TING
THE CREATIVE
DIRECTOR
THANK YOU
KONNECTING THE
TING LONDON

TEHO
was here!

THIS IS FINE

Living Within Your Memes

Remixing popular memes. I spend way too much time on the internet. But including these to end the lectures was always fun.

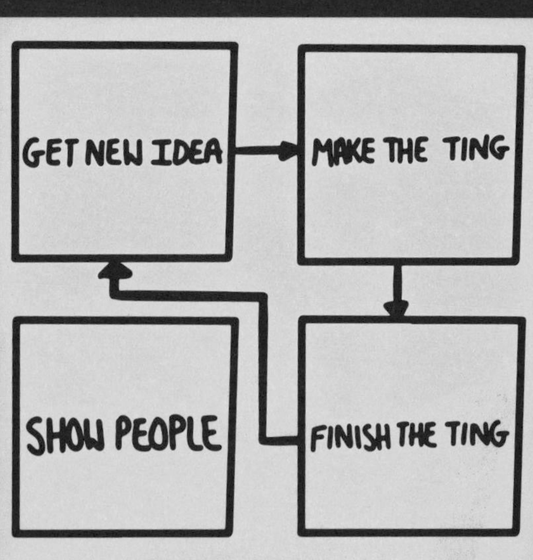

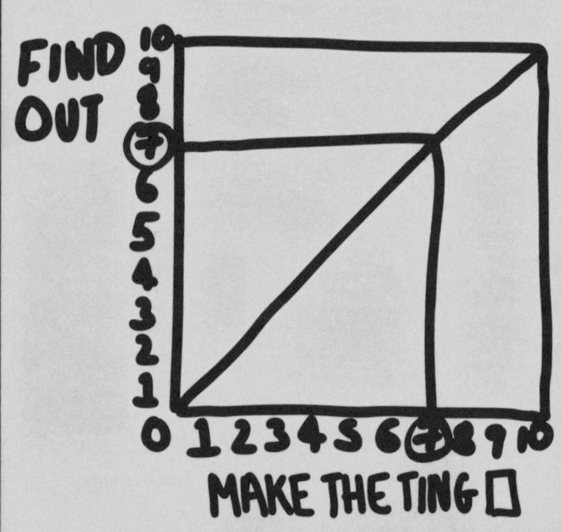

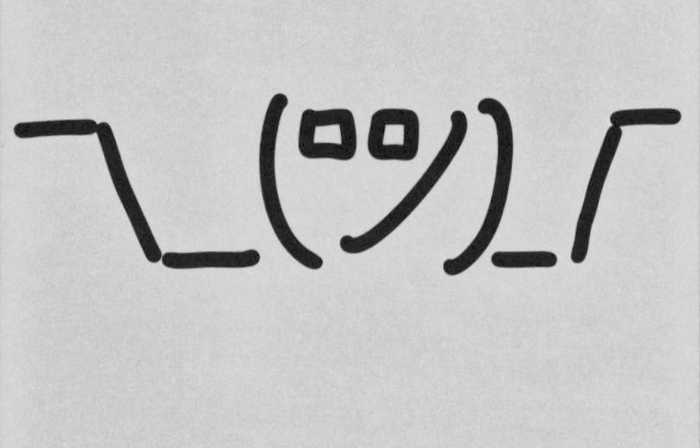

"Close the app, make the ting"
"If you love music you should learn how to dj"
"The man dem didn't put the aerials up for this"
"Rent is the creative director"
"Name an artist that has made more than 100 songs you love"
"Remix the ting"
"Friends buy tickets"
"Are the ideas still true at scale?"
"Deep Feedback"
"1/1 > #1"
"So anti Algo it might bang"
"You should apply for grant funding"
"Imposter syndrome is a feature not a bug"
"There aren't enough DJs"
"Test the process"
"Formats are the new genres"
"Art is making writhin your means"
"You don't need a marketing plan"
"Drink water before you log in"
"Maybe the music isn't good enough"
"More people writing about music is good for music"
"High follower count is becoming a negative indicator"
"It takes a village to raise an artist"
"The camera roll is the mood board"
"Dance is the physical embodiment of optimism"
"Document your ting"
"Social media is a canvas"

The Mandem Didn't Put Up The Aerials For This!

A reflection on the state of British music, in particular Black British music in June 2024. I printed some t shirts with the statement on the back, but I flipped it and made a special edition set of t-shirts for artists I rate, with 'What the man dem put up the aerials for' instead, The version pictured was for Jim Legxacy and his project 'Black British Music (2024).

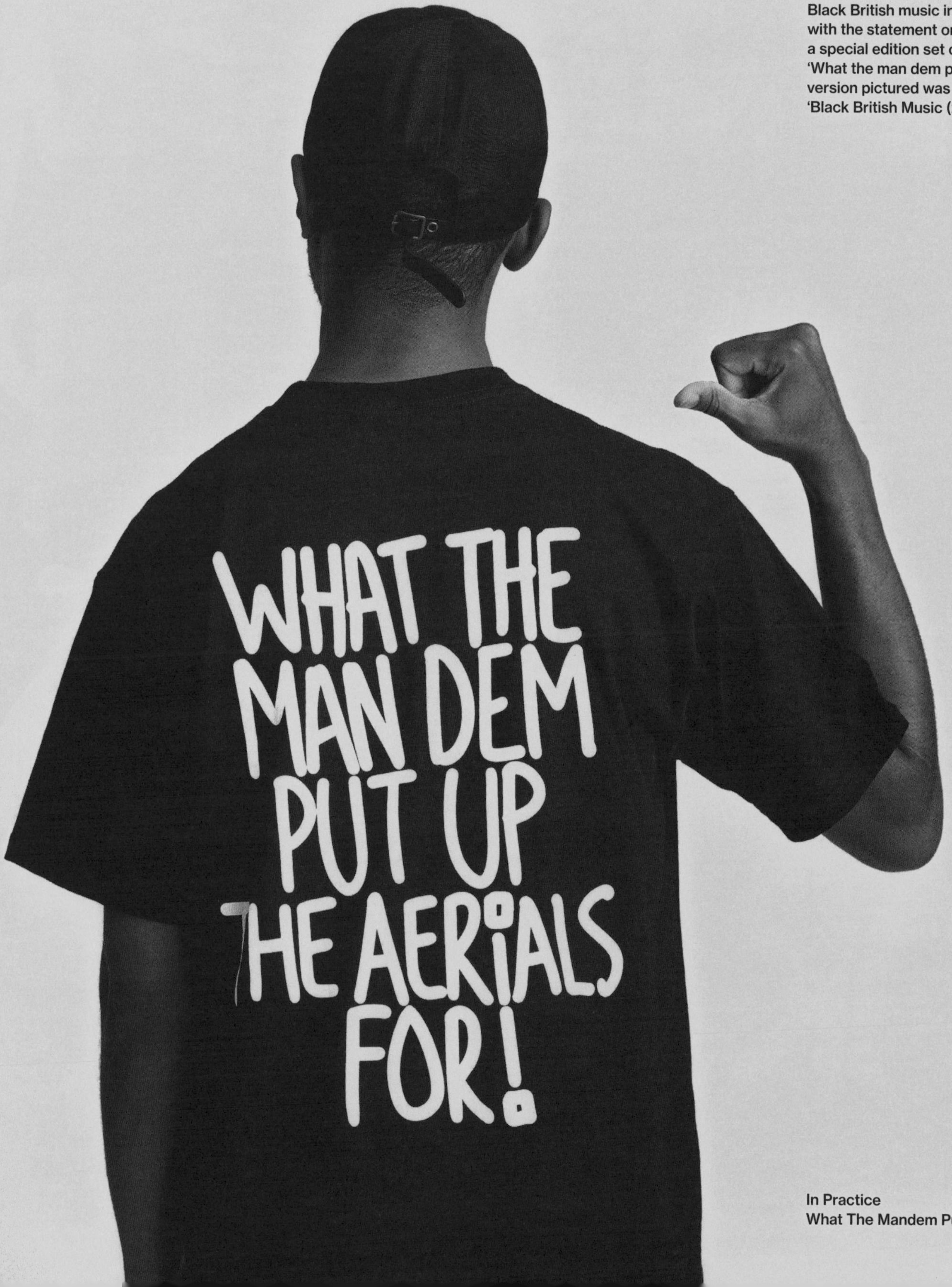

In Practice
What The Mandem Put Up The Aerials For!

THE MAN DEM DIDN'T PUT UP THE AERIALS FOR THIS!

If You Love Music You Should Learn How To DJ
Lecture

If you love music, you should learn how to DJ: The Lecture - AVA Festival, London and FWB Fest in California. The definition of a DJ has been rigid for way too long, and I've used these lectures to explore the idea of what a DJ is in a world of infinite content. I think this is book number two, so I used these lectures as a way to showcase the work in progress.

DJING HAS BEEN ___________ HISTORICALLY. NOW TECHNOLOGY HAS CHANGED IT CAN BE ___________.

ANALOGUE
FOR THE VIBES
DIGITAL
FOR THE TOOLS

Digital For The Tools, Analogue For The Vibes

Worked on a project with the Vinyl Alliance to bring a group of artists together to visit The Vinyl Factory pressing plant in Hayes to learn about the record making process, and press a record for themselves. We all pressed our own copy of Yaw Evans remix of 'Start With Why' from my album, in April 2024. If you ever find one, keep it offline!

Rave The Ting

Big respect to promoters. It's hard thankless work. You have to be crazy to do it. Rave The Ting in Queens Yard was sick. Rave The Ting in Village Underground got cancelled before we could even put the tickets on sale. Cool idea though, and Melly designed the characters as part of the flyers.

RAVE THE TING
RAMON SUCESSO
HAGAN MELLY
ELIJAH & JAMMZ

VILLAGEUNDERGROUND
OCT 4TH 2024

RAVE! THE TING
MAY 4TH 2024 QUEENS YARD
MANJ · MIA KODEN
YAW EVANS
ELIJAH & SKILLIAM

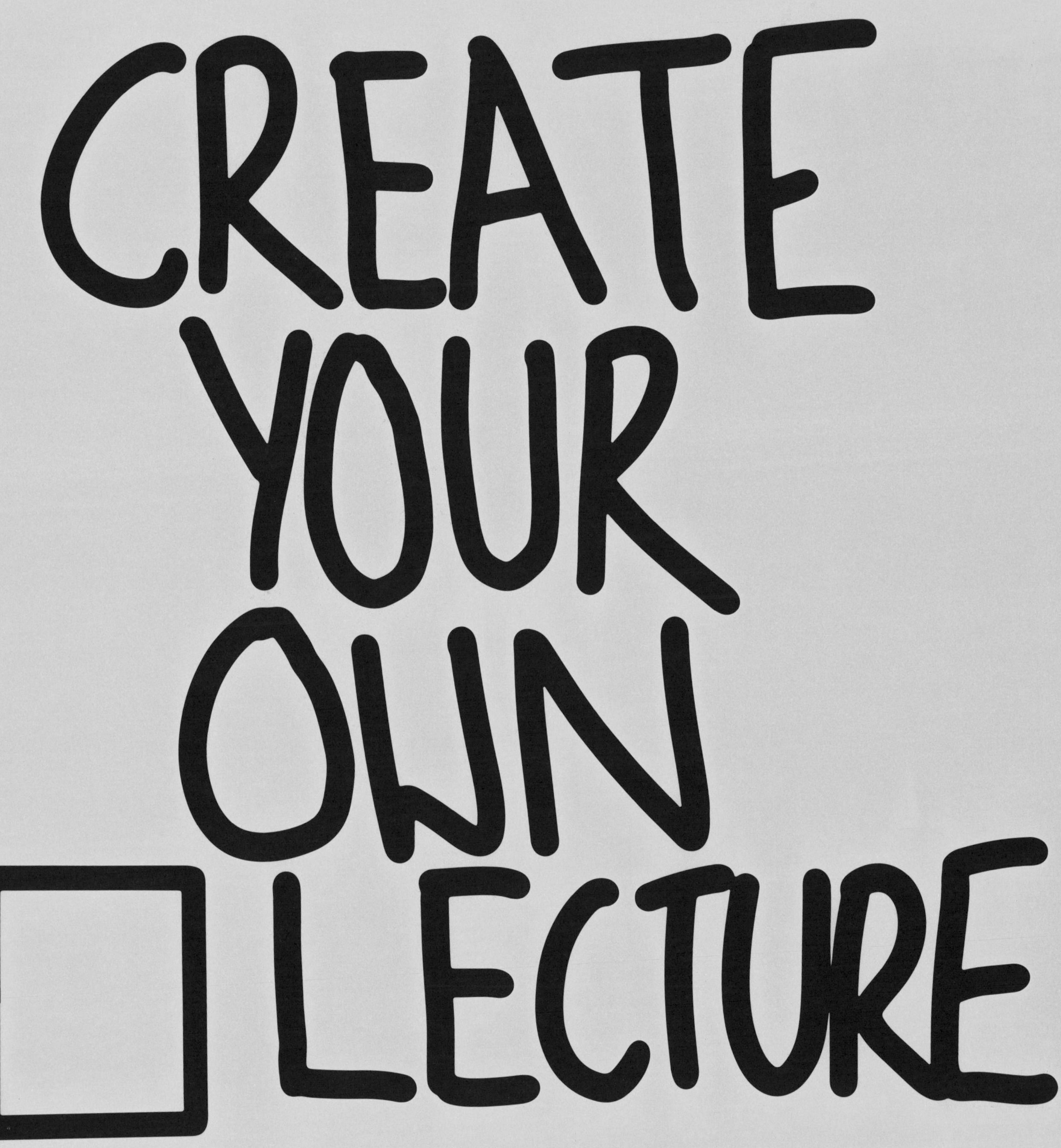
CREATE
YOUR
OWN
LECTURE

Create Your Own Lecture

The lectures have been the main vessel for developing the ideas in this project. Having to answer questions in real life about the ideas help shake out the weak ones, and make me commit to the strong ones and develop stand alone projects out of them. A by-product of this that I didn't intend is people taking pictures of the squares they like during the lectures, and sharing them on their pages.

This is 10x more effective than just panels with a few people talking. If I ran conferences I wouldn't have any panels. Just highly prepared lectures, then breaks for everyone to talk and some music to break it up. I can never remember what anyone says when there's more than two people talking too. Panels won't change the world. Create your own lectures. This tweet trolling me from 2019 ended up coming true.

EVEN IF IT'S CREDITED TO ONE PERSON, MOST GREAT SONGS ARE COLLABORATIONS

DIFFICULT TO PURSUE A CAREER IN THE ARTS IF NOBODY TELLS YOU HOW THEY EARN A LIVING

CONNECTION > ENGAGEMENT

Flowdem Skeng

SAYING THE WORD 'LOVE' TO THE MAN DEM IS GOOD FOR EVERYONES MENTAL HEALTH

GIVE US MUCH CONTEXT FOR FINANCIAL OFFERS TO FREELANCERS. IF ASKING FOR FREE LABOUR, EXPLAIN WHY.

BEING A FULL TIME ARTIST DOESN'T MEAN YOUR WORK IS 'BETTER' THAN ANYONE ELSES

THE ALGORITHM IS A GATEKEEPER

IF I KNEW WHAT WAS GOING TO 'WORK', I'D DO THAT INSTEAD OF WRITING THIS

'DO WHAT YOU DID BEFORE' IS ONE OF THE MOST UNHELPFUL THINGS YOU CAN SAY TO AN ARTIST

IT WASN'T 'REAL'
DJING WITHOUT VINYL
RADIO WITHOUT FM
JOURNALISM WITHOUT PRINT

IF YOU DON'T DO SOMETHING YOU WANT TO DO CREATIVELY BECAUSE OF A WHAT IF SCENARIO... DO IT UNTIL THE SCENARIO HAPPENS

BEING ABLE TO ASK QUESTIONS AND BEING ASKED A LOT OF QUESTIONS HAS HELPED ME MORE THAN ADVICE

CULTURE WAS THE WORD OF THE 10s COMMUNITY IS THE WORD OF THE 20s

ONCE YOU RELEASE A SONG IT BECOMES OPEN SOURCE

HIGH SHIPPING COSTS, TAXES & BREXIT WILL BE THE DEATH OF VINYL FOR SMALL LABELS

AN ARTIST NAME YOU CAN TRADEMARK WILL MAKE THINGS EASIER

YOU HAVE TO WORK OUT IF WHOEVER IS CRITIQUING YOU WANTS YOU TO DO 'BETTER' OR JUST THEIR WAY

EVERYTIME YOU MAKE FOR A PLATFORM YOU DON'T OWN MAKE FOR ONE YOU DO

KNOW THE DIFFERENCE BETWEEN CANNOT BE DONE AND HASN'T BEEN DONE

BRITISH SONGS WITH THE WORD 'BANDO'
2000 2010 2022

YOU DON'T KNOW WHEN GOOD A&R HAPPENS. YOU THINK YOU KNOW WHEN BAD A&R HAPPENS

FUN EXPERIMENT IF YOU MAKE A LOT OF MUSIC: FOR EACH RELEASE DO ONE FORMAT I.E STREAMING, NFTs BANDCAMP etc SEE WHAT CONNECTS...

COMMUNITIES
ARTISTS
GATEKEEPERS

WHAT ARE THE JOBS OF THE FUTURE IN MUSIC & CULTURE?

HOW MUCH SHOULD YOU BE PAID PER STREAM?

I PREFER 'LAUNCH' TO 'DROP' ONE IS THE START ONE IS THE END

THE BEST THING ABOUT GOING TO A LECTURE OR PANEL IS MEETING NEW PEOPLE INTO THE SAME IDEAS

END OF YEAR LISTS SHOULD BE MORE SPECIFIC. GIVE US A VERSE THATS MOVED YOU

"FREEDOM FROM THE KNOWN"
Mala

HARDEST PART OF MANAGEMENT: MANAGING EXPECTATIONS

YOUR NICHE ISN'T AS BIG AS YOUR FEED MAKES IT FEEL.

WOULD YOU RATHER BE AN ARTIST 100 YEARS AGO, 1000 YEARS AGO, 10,000 YEARS AGO OR TODAY?

YOU DO NOT WORK FOR YOUR AGENT. YOU ARE PARTNERS

TWO CAREER ARTIST PATHS:
1. NOT BE BORING
2. SERVE PEOPLE WHAT THEY WANT
3. MAKE UP YOUR OWN PATH

IF YOU ENJOY SOMEONES WORK TRY NOT TO PROJECT WHAT YOU THINK THEY SHOULD BE ON TO THEM

NTS 1 LDN
RAJ B2B + AMA ELIJAH
FRIDAY 13.5.22
1300-1500

READING THE ROOM > ASKING THE AUDIENCE

Grime is what you make it!
Royal-T

3 Flats
E3

A GOOD SONG HAS ALWAYS BEEN UNDERPRICED

ITS A COMPLIMENT FOR SOMEONE TO REMEMBER ART YOU HAVE CREATED IN THIS FAST MOVING WORLD

CAPTURING A MOMENT DOESN'T MEAN YOU NEED TO PUBLISH THAT MOMENT

WHAT DO YOU THINK THE MAJORITY ARE WRONG ABOUT?

HOW DIFFERENT WOULD UK MUSIC BE IF THE WEALTHIEST ARTISTS FUNDED OTHER ARTISTS WITH NO STRINGS?

YOU ARE VERY SMART OR VERY LUCKY IF YOU HAVEN'T HAD TO CHANGE YOUR MIND ABOUT WHAT YOU WORK ON OR BELIEVE IN SINCE 2020

ALL COMMERCIAL SUCCESS IN ART IS AN ANOMALY

HOW ATTACHED ARE YOU TO YOUR ARTIST NAME?

WHAT ARE YOU WORKING ON THAT PEOPLE DON'T SEE, THAT IS INFLUENCING YOUR WORK?

WHAT DO YOU LIKE THAT ISN'T ALREADY POPULAR?

TRYING TO BUY AN AUDIENCE WILL BANKRUPT YOU CREATIVELY & FINANCIALLY

ARE THEY TELLING YOU THEIR FINDINGS OR READING YOU THE NEWS?

ARE YOU GETTING ADVICE OR A HISTORY LESSON?

DOES THE PERSON KNOW ENOUGH ABOUT YOU TO GIVE YOU GOOD ADVICE?

WHEN I STARTED UNI IN 2005 THEY CALLED THE SAME OLD SCHOOL GARAGE YOU CALL OLD SCHOOL GARAGE NOW OLD SCHOOL GARAGE

SOME CREATIVE WORK IS HARD BECAUSE IT ISNT WHAT YOU SHOULD WORK ON RIGHT NOW

INDEPENDENCE IS ORGANIC. INDEPENDENCE IS ADULT EDUCATION.

ARTIST SHOWCASE CONFERENCES ARE A RELIC. WE HAVE MORE DATA THAN EVER THAT TALENT BUYERS + LABELS CAN USE. DISCOVERY IS 24/7 ON SOCIALS.

IS THERE A LACK OF OPPORTUNITY OR A NARROW VIEW OF OPPORTUNITY?

IT MIGHT BE BETTER TO SAY YOU DON'T UNDERSTAND SOMETHING ARTISTICALLY RATHER THAN DISLIKING IT.

ENDING TINGS IS AS IMPORTANT AS STARTINGS TINGS

Ending Tings

Without the opportunity to end the project on my own terms, it will either fizzle out because of my lack of enthusiasm, get repetitive, or the platforms will adjust in a way that no longer favours this kind of content. Before any of those things happen, compiling it, celebrating it, and moving on is a necessary part of the creative process.

Stopping gives room for the ideas in the squares to become projects of their own. Reading them all back, there are ideas for books, documentaries, songs, albums, raves and businesses. I will only get to do a few, so I need to make sure I make time to do them, rather than just talking about them.

A lot of the creative blocks I've experienced have come from sticking to an idea for too long. This is art, we can start with a clean canvas every single day if we want to.

Thank You

It took a village to raise me, so this won't begin to cover the amount of people that have had part in this project coming together, but first wanted to shout out two pillars.

Mum, for giving me the space to create. There has been a lot of talk about what 'privilege' means in the creative world, and having a supportive home environment gave me a significant head start in life. Being able to stay at home while I figured things out, in a culturally rich environment was the second layer of privilege. Being able to open up our home so people could stay while they figured out things changed a few lives too. The generosity I learned from you is something I've tried to continue in my own way through all of my creative work.

I've been lucky enough to have a consistent friendship, creative relationship and business partnership with Skilliam for the last 17 years, and that is the bedrock that all of this is built on. He does the unfashionable work that is under-appreciated in this industry, behind the scenes, taking care of the business, logistics and royalties for our artist projects. Without him none of this is possible. He's made sure we've been able to remain lean, and his foresight has helped us avoid disaster many times. The credit I get for my work is all split equally with Skilliam.

Eternal love to all of these people for reasons that I could dedicate an entire page to each. The Butterz Core: Royal-T, Swindle, Flava D, DJ Q, David Kelly.

My people that have been close to me through this period: Alicia, Dane, April, Leo, Alex, Dan, Sam, Julie, Max, Mike, CESRV, Andy, Andres, Sophia, Ed, Angela, Freshta, Chand, Inie, Logan, Bobby, Phoebe, Despa, Emma and Jammz.

Shout out to Mike Calandra, Daniel Williams, Caspar Melville, Alli Beddoes, Juha Van't Zelfde and Tom Dodd for believing in me at important junctions in my life.

Colin from Velocity for making the book happen.
Alfie for designing it!

Jubilee for suggesting I put my ideas from Twitter onto Instagram!

Buitumelo for inspiring the name of the book!

Thank you to everyone who's supported my work and ideas through sharing, commenting, coming to a lecture or a rave, but most importantly thank you to the artists past, present and future for inspiring me to Close The App, Make The Ting.

Elijah

THANK YOU!

CLOSE
THE
APP
MAKE
THE
FING
BIG SIX

TO ROB THANK YOU
FOR MAKING SPACE
FOR ALL OF US TO
MAKE TINGS TEN87
X FOREVER
MUCH LOVE
ELIJAH !
SEP 30 2023!?

CLOSE
THE
APP
MAKE
THE
THING

CLOSE THE APP
MAKE THE THING
@MAKE THE TING

ELIJAH!
GUEST LECTURE
BREAK FREE
FEB 11TH 2023 8PM
ARCAN

THE ENDZ
IS A
CANVAS

giprint
THING

THE WORD IN THE 10'S
WAS CULTURE
THE WORD IN THE 20'S
IS COMMUNITY
WHAT WILL BE THE
OF THE 30'S?

THERE IS
ONLY ONE
OCTOBER 21ST 2023
TIME IS THE
CREATIVE
DIRECTOR
DON'T TRUST
THE PROCESS

TIME IS THE
CREATIVE
DIRECTOR

CLOSE THE APP
MAKE THE THING
@MAKE THE TING

CLOSE
THE
APP
MAKE
THE
TING

← Studios
Offices →
DON'T TRUST THE
PROCESS, TEST
THE PROCESS

SOCIAL MEDIA IS A CANVAS
JAZZ IS A CANVAS
LIFE IS A CANVAS!
BREAK FREE!

TIME IS THE
CREATIVE
DIRECTOR

THANK YOU FOR HAVING ME
BEN IT'S BEEN A PLEASURE!
FRIENDS
BUY
HOCKLEY HUSTLE
TICKETS

MAN LIKE ALEX
HAPPY BIRTHDAY!
DOCUMENT YOUR
TING, LIFE, VIBE
WRITTEN BY @ELIJAH NOV 3RD 2023
BIG UP FOR BEING A GREAT
FRIEND. MORE LIFE
@MAKETHEBUMBACLATTING

ASH
CLOSE
THE
APP
MAKE

THE FIRST
ARTIST
I EVER
MET!

JULY 30TH 2024 I FOUND
@AVIEW.FROMABRIDGE
JULY 31ST JOE FILMED
ON ENDZ. TOPICS
EAST LONDON, PIRA
RADIO, 'THE CULTU
DOCUMENTING OUR TING!
BIG UP BRUV @ELIJAH

CLOSE THE APP
MAKE THE THING

THE MANDEM
DON'T KNEEL!
CONGRATULATIONS
IWGP WORLD CHAMP
ZACK SABRE J

ELIJAH!
GUEST LECTURE
CLOSE THE APP
MAKE THE THING
A GOOD IDEA IN LONDON OR BERLIN MAY NOT BE A GOOD IDEA IN ____
IT'S A CREATIVE ECOSYSTEM WHEN EVERYONE IS BUILDING DIFF IDEAS WITH THE SAME PRINCIPLES
1/1 > #1
SOCIAL MEDIA IS A CANVAS
IMPOSTER SYNDROME IS A FEATURE NOT A BUG
BREAK FREE
DON'T TRUST THE PROCESS TEST THE PROCESS
THINK LOCAL + ACT LOCAL + SHARE ONLINE
FEB 11TH 2023 8PM!
ARCAN

THINK OUTSIDE
THE

CLOSE
THE
APP
MAKE
THE
TING

CLOSE
THE
APP
MAKE
THE

KEEP
HUSH

LIVE
ON STAGE
DJs
ARE
MUSIC
JOURNALISTS

CLOSE
THE
APP
MAKE
THE
TING

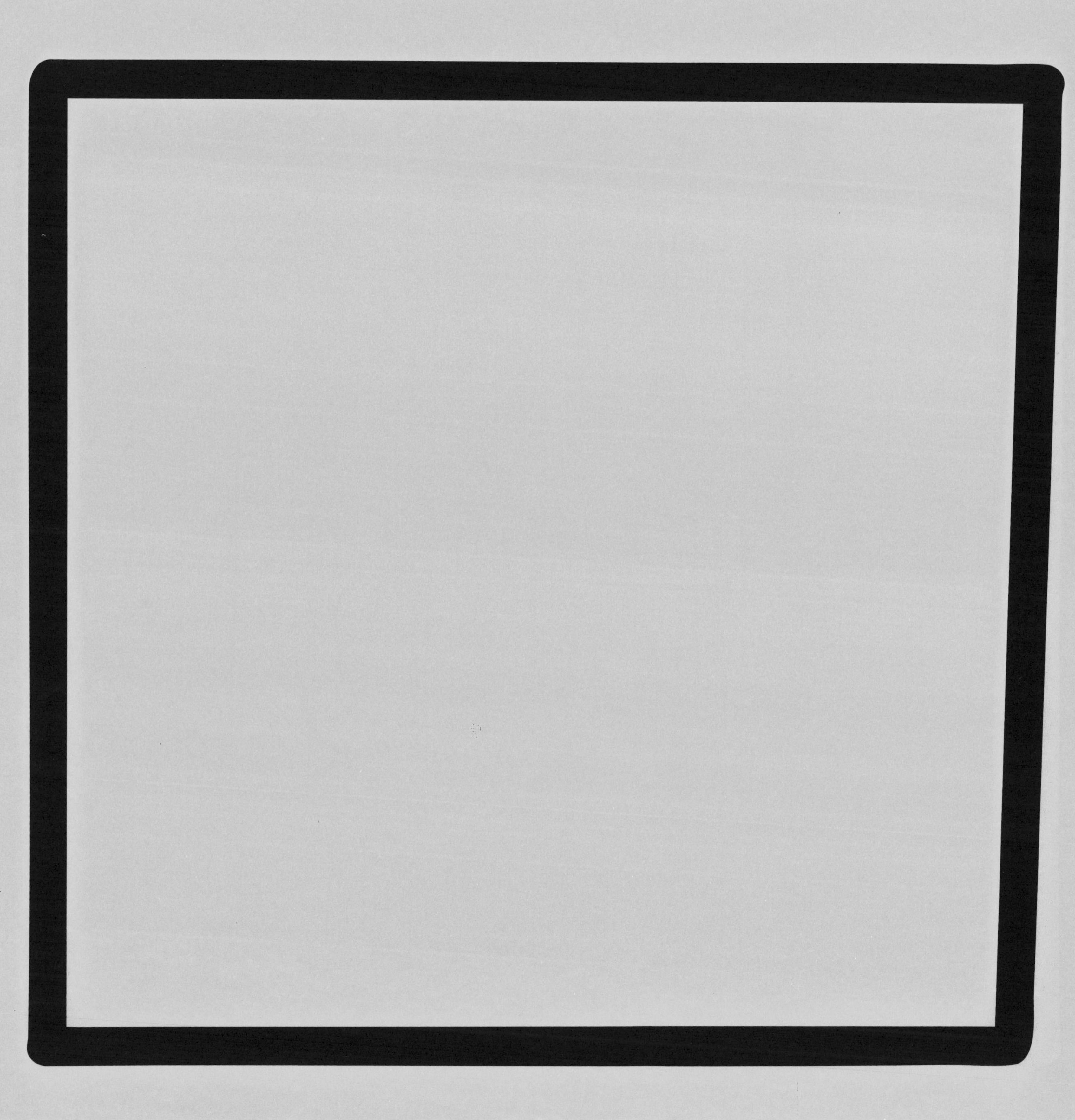

Who Made The Ting

www.velocitypress.uk

Artworks and words: Elijah
Graphic Design: Alfie Allen & Max Marshall
Editor: Colin Steven

ISBN: 978-1-913231-79-8
Printed in Poland by Interlak